Elementary Verse

Eve Killip

authorHOUSE®

AuthorHouse™ UK Ltd.
500 Avebury Boulevard
Central Milton Keynes, MK9 2BE
www.authorhouse.co.uk
Phone: 08001974150

© 2009 Eve Killip. All rights reserved.

No part of this book may be reproduced, stored in a retrieval system, or transmitted by any means without the written permission of the author.

First published by AuthorHouse 5/4/2009

ISBN: 978-1-4389-5566-7 (sc)

Printed in the United States of America
Bloomington, Indiana

This book is printed on acid-free paper.

Acknowledgements

I would like to say a heart felt thank you to Bobbie, my daughter, for putting up with all my woeful witterings while I was compiling this book. I couldn't have done without her support, and in particular, with her computing skills.

Contents

Air	1
Fire	2
Water	3
Earth	4
Middle Aged Adolescence	5
Either Side of Nice	6
The Palate of a Rural Scene	7
Daughters of Eve	8
Arch Enemies	9
St. Audrie's Bay	10
What if bread had never been invented?	11
Hell Fire	12
The Age of Sex	13
Aloneness	14
The Chains Within	15
Ephemeral Presence	16
Young and Easy, in Love	17
She's Making It Up	18
Mind Over Body or Perhaps Body Over Mind	19
Abstinence Makes the Lust Grow Stronger	20
Doodles in the Dark	21
Dream	22
Strange Feline Habits	23

Blind Faith	24
St. Mary's	25
Elation 3	26
Red	27
Flying the Nest	29
Returning From the Sea	31
Guitar	32
Above	33
Techno Canticle	34
The Mystical Road Home	35
Solitude While Travelling	36
Rural night	38
The Rites of Passage Trilogy	39
Mindscape	40
Ideas thief	41
Beautiful bed	42
Vivaldi's 4 Seasons	43
Daemon of Doubt	44
For the lack of a quack	45
Desirability	46
Coffee broken	47
Inebriate Observations	48
Head way	49
Rainbow	50
Slugduggery	51
Rhythms of the World	52

Air

The overseer of thought,
Inspiration and idea bearer,
The creator of beginnings,
Yet hardly there at all.

Air brings music,
Rhythm and melody,
Sounds carried aloft,
Supported perfectly.

Air gives us oxygen,
The exact amount.
Makes breathing unnoticeable,
For us, plants and animals.

Spirits of the air dance,
Sylphs have freedom of the sky,
Freshness of ozone,
Bourne on the wind.

Air is of childhood,
And spring abounds,
Aether invisibly binds our world,
Making magic happen.

Fire

Flame,
Dancing,
Red,
Radiating,
Hot,
With energy.

Action,
Change,
Therefore magic.
Passion,
Sacred sex,
The spark of divinity.

Within,
Waiting for the signal,
Now. – Act now,
Before the spark dies,
Let it come...
Dare.

Water

Rushing, gushing or dripping,
The force of water.
Spiral movement
Filling the lowest space.

Yin, water and ice,
Yang, can transform to steam.
Water remembers,
Vibrations and electromagnetically.

Spirits of water, playful,
Children are fascinated,
Pouring water,
Hearing it splash.

Swimming gives freedom of movement,
Helps us breathe well and gain stamina,
Health can be attained,
If we let the spirits of water help.

Water brings life to earth,
Nourishing dry lands,
It is the life blood of the Goddess,
Without it our planet would be barren.

Earth

Earth seems the eternal giver,
And people take.
She gives us a home
And a place to roam.

Earth feeds our bellies,
And feasts our eyes.
Satisfies our senses,
And people exploit.

Earth is patient,
And people are not.
Human greed invents,
Sometimes unnecessarily so.

And then sometimes we get it right,
And it feels so good.
Being 'in tune' with nature
Makes us feel nurtured.

To look after earth is not a chore,
Let her waters run clear,
Her forests thrive,
It helps us all to be alive.

Middle Aged Adolescence

Do you think it right
Do you think I should
Sow wild oats in middle age?
Such things are associated with
The young,
Being free and having fun.

But freedom was never mine,
When I should have had the time
Of my life,
I was a wife
For Gods sake
Trouble and strife
For Gods sake
Haunted me year on year.

Now I'm ready with open mind
To let go the ties that bind
I'm ready to find my own way
And if you think I'm going astray
Well, that's your problem.

Either Side of Nice

Opposites
Man and woman
Or a disunited one?

Opposites
Left and right
Or extremes of equilibrium.

Opposites
Black and white
Is grey only middling?

Opposites
Up and down
Which would hovering be?

Opposites
Good and bad
Now here's the moral weighting –

Is good all good
And bad all bad;
And if there were a half way point
Wouldn't that be NICE?

The Palate of a Rural Scene

A road of mud and stone
Runs around my home.
Cottages predating mine
Sit opposite and recline
Into the landscape beyond.

The roofs are of grey slate
And an uneven pitch.
Chimney pots stand, some six in a row
Issuing smoke from fires below
Which dissipates into the wide immense sky.

The walls of these cottages
Are painted, some cream, some beige
All blending with the green backdrop
Of broadleaved trees and a shock
Of yellow flowers
Brilliant against the subdued house colours.

Late evening and the sky, the palest of blue
Another hue.
Birds sing unseen. Two horses
Riders aloft trot past
A cat strolls by, easy.

Sundown, it feels like time
To sup a glass of deep red wine,
Feel the day giving way
To night times' blackened dome
When silver moonshine rests upon my home.

Daughters of Eve

She needs her lover
She needs his strength
His arms to encircle her
Dispelling tension.

She needs her lover
To take control
To allow her soul
To surface.

She needs her lover
As soil needs rain
To yield the forbidden fruit
He ripens.

Taking her pair in his hands
Devouring them
Until he extracts her juice
From the sweet, sweet centre.

She needs her lover
To open her body
To let go the frenzy
That's tied up inside her.
To let it all come
Wave after wave
So strong, so strong
She needs
Fucking.

Arch Enemies

The battles overlap, ensue.

Housework and I, never had a good relationship.
I never learned the art of keeping house.
But it's there constantly – housework.
It resides in my home and never leaves.
It must be agoraphobic.
Perhaps I should make allowances,
But I don't,
Won't.
It makes me do things I hate,
Like... empty cupboards and then put it all back again.
Futile.

It makes me buy far more food than necessary
Just so that it's cupboards are well stocked.

Housework is such a hard task master.
Relentlessly presenting one job after another.
It tries to impose a routine on me
So far it's failed
Tee hee hee.

Housework seems to have the ability
To make work multiply.
It makes me see the next job
Before I've finished the one I'm doing.
It likes to stretch into the future
It likes me to know that it will always be there
It likes the doom of permanence.

But tomorrow I'll have my respite
I'm going on holiday, leaving housework behind;
I hope it'll be lonely.

St. Audrie's Bay

St. Audrie's Bay
Where the rocks do lay,
In soft colours
And formation.
The wind, a gentle breeze
Wraps itself with clinging ease
Seducing you to stay a little longer.

The waves are small
And never tall.

The sea has stripes of deep and shallow,
The patterns change with the ripples
Tide and sun and shadow;
And way out deep
A tune, a rhythm
Fills the air
And rocky schism.

What if bread had never been invented?

What would you spread your marmalade on?
And imagine breakfast without toast,
Think how messy sandwiches would be
If bread had never been invented.

The art of bread making wouldn't be known
No proving or kneading or knocking back
And chefs' hats might be flat, like caps
If bread had never been invented.

Bread and butter pudding would be just butter pudding
And eggy bread unheard of,
So many of lives little comforts would be missing
If bread had never been invented.

Mother would have nothing to be proud of
And the smell of baking bread is something to be missed,
And all those best things since slicing, may not be
If bread had never been invented.

Hell Fire

I lit a small fire in the grate
And on it threw the things I hate
Written on small pieces of card
I watched the words burn until they were chard.

Needless stupidity, gone in a flame,
Patheticness ended the same,
Waste and greed, blackened and burned
I threw them away, are the lessons learned?

They made small flames red, blue and yellow
They created a warmth and a heartening glow.
Strange to think that such comfort can come
From attitudes that create a pain in the bum.

The Age of Sex

8.30, I've been stood up
It's quite funny really
At my age
9.30, I've been stood up
What's wrong with me
At my age?
Perhaps he doesn't like
My style of dress
The woman on his arm
At my age
Perhaps he doesn't like
The folds around my waist,
That happens when you get
To my age –
Perhaps he's shallow enough
To need a 20 year old
At his age
But she won't understand
That if he can't make it
It isn't his fault, at his age.

Aloneness

Lonely? No!!
Me, myself and I
Keep each other company.
We go for walks
Or watch T.V.
And write silly poetry.

Life is full
We tell ourselves, with
Meditation, intoxication
Nicotine inhalation.
Wishful thinking – fornication.
Oh woe are we
For the need to be
In other human company.

The Chains Within

Sometimes I want to be alone
Go somewhere, be on my own,
But then a fear creeps into me –
It prevents me from being free.

Sometimes the fear is in my mind,
Sometimes it's within mankind,
I want to go beyond, but then
Something brings me back again.

If I were brave enough to roam
And leave the safety of my home,
Perhaps I'd taste the truth, and see
The meaning of reality.

Ephemeral Presence

The impermanence of foot prints in the sand
Taken by the sea from the land.
Now no evidence to suggest her ubiety at all
But the pattern of the waves stays in her head
The tempo, the order unceasing
Every seventh wave smaller and quieter than the rest;
It always knows where to stop.

Young and Easy, in Love

Her love came too easily
In the past,
Perhaps it wasn't deep enough
It didn't last.
It changed from love to
Something other,
She found she had a husband,
Not a lover.

She's Making It Up

All art is contrived
But what is art?
These words? Surely not!
But they are fashioned
Moulded, borrowed, stolen
By fair means or foul
In innocence or not.
What have you got?
A set of lines
Maybe a poem,
New, novel?
From me, yes
Original?
These questions must
Have been asked already.
But like Mutt's Fontaine 1917
Is it art?

Mind Over Body
or Perhaps Body Over Mind

Thoughts in blue
Of you
It might be true
It could be love.
Does that mean monotony
Or do I mean monogamy.

Am I down on my luck?
I could do with a ...
Beer
To bring me some cheer.

But these ways
Of single days
Will become history
Just a mystery.
Should I succumb?
Would I be undone?

But oh those thoughts in blue.

Abstinence Makes the Lust Grow Stronger

Smooth, sensual, spunky, seductive,

Energetic, erotic, erogenous, enslaved,

Xciting, xhilerating, x rated, xhausting

YES.

Doodles in the Dark

Doodles in the dark,
They did it for a lark.
Kids in youthful innocence
Screamed in knowledge and pretence.
Some raised a shout
Some sounded brave,
Made silly jokes
But this isn't a rave,
It's just a hoax.

On Monday night
The lights went down
All was quiet within the town.
Was it Rikkie, was it James
Made hooting noises in the lanes.

But it had all been a fix
Even though it was a risk,
The wires were cut and blamed on road works.
Who knows what in the bushes lurks?
Plunged us into a great blind panic
But you're the ones labelled – manic.

Dream

The thoughts of one dream
And the scene of another
Merged and overlapped.

I remember thinking that I couldn't breath,
I wanted to lie down but I was at work,
I wanted to drive home but felt too tired.

A familiar voice was telling me
That I ought to go and rest,
I couldn't decide what to do.

Then before me was a strange scene in sepia
Of two children kneeling as if in prayer,
And an elegant woman danced by me.
I don't know who she was, or the children
Come to that.

Then a constant rhythm of ringing
Woke me. "Hello".
A call to tell me that the friend
I was about to meet was ill, with the
Symptoms of my dream.

Strange Feline Habits

Paper must be sat on
No matter how small
It must be sat on.
Then sometimes it's the enemy
And must be destroyed at all cost.

Carrier bags have the same fascination.

The cat flap has to be stared at
Intently and for ages.
"Have you forgotten how it works?"
"What do you expect it to do"
... A strange cat habit.

Then there's the patch of sunlight,
It's compulsory for cats to sit in it.
To tuck all four paws under them
Let their eyelids droop
And grin a silly grin.

Ritualistic cleaning
Another feline oddity.
Methodically working from back legs to front
And fastidiously licking between the toes,
If you're a cat, that's how it goes.

Best of all finding a lap,
We humans have our uses.
Jump up and pummel a few times
Turn right round, then lie down
Curl around, purr deeply
Sleep sweetly.

Blind Faith

You invited me in
But it was black inside,
I was clumsy and unsure.
The years have taught you well
You have learned to tell
The difference in temperature
Pressure, sounds and texture.

Your fingers sense
With the lightest touch.
Your memory stores
How things feel and sound;
It's a new world to me
Cos my eyes always see
But you've shown me
That eyes can deceive.

You've opened a door
I know that there's more
And seeing isn't always believing;
 Things smooth and things rough
Ungiving and soft
Can be sensed tactily.

I'll be your eyes
But they're not always so wise.
Your world was such a surprise.

St. Mary's

The golden solidity punctuates the village end,
Or announces it's beginning.
Making a statement big and bold
Just as the houses are thinning.

Enormous keyholes announce
The spaciousness inside
And there the calmness envelopes
It's a place where you can hide.

Golden stone from fields around,
And windows, many, let light flood in
Arranged as if to drive away
Erroneous ways and village sin.

Arches of door and window line
And those within point Godwards.
Walls of white and columns make
A model cathedral of our times.

Castellating and buttress lend fabric
And gargoyle misses not a trick.
Stonemasons did you work with humour
Or is this just another rumour.

In the grounds the graves erected
But alas few names detected,
Excepting for Mary Arnold
Whose yew tree your name upholds.

Weather vane on tower square,
St. Mary watches all is fair,
Prayer and whimsical and whim.
Reflected gladly in your hymn.

Elation 3

Bobbie made a sculpture
Of an ambiguous kind,
She said it was two people
But perhaps had bed in mind.

Inspiration was elation
A level headed thought
But one is higher than the other
Meaning next to nought.

The people are quite abstract
But pleased to see each other.
Their shape is very similar
The difference is their colour.

These happy seeming people
Cast in clay for ever.
The Levellers said they want to
See it – well I never!

But alas they didn't buy it
Didn't even want to try it.
They said they didn't understand,
Fame and fortune quick as sand.

Red

Red on red
Blood in flames
Temper flares
Then lowly glows.

Life and spirit the colour of red
Love in bed
Remember what was said.

Red, the colour of speed
Flashing metallic energy
Hurries past
Fast.

Pillar box red
It's a red letter day
A final demand
That's what it says.
Writing a cheque
With ink that is red
It may as well be blood
But what the heck.

My account's in the red
But that's only money
There's an aura of red
Isn't it funny.

The colour of energy
Leaves me feeling knackered
But I don't paint my nails
And my hair ain't lacquered.

Much more of this I just can't take
Where's it leading to, for goodness sake,
The little red rooster woke me this morning
Just started crowing, gave me no warning.

I'm so tired now I'm off to bed
But I won't close my eyes cos I'm filled with dread
I might dream a dream in the colour red.

Flying the Nest

You gave us your love
And we flourished.
A happy girl and boy
Secure in the family structure.

But you gave us your thoughts
And conditions
Reining us in
To be seen and not heard.

Perhaps you weren't aware
That when the umbilical cord is cut
We find our own path
Needing only guidance, not granite chiselled rules.

Well here we are now
And maybe I'm not the daughter you wanted,
Perhaps I'm not the mother I should have been,
But the me has emerged.

I had to take flight,
Cut loose the reins.
Bolt, though the stable door
Was only open a crack.

But the reins seemed to stretch for miles,
My thoughts weren't my own,
I still conferred
As, I thought, acknowledging your superiority.

Was that what you wanted?
Or did I get it wrong?
Were you longing for the day
When you had no more responsibility for me?

Well the day has come –
I take full responsibility for myself and my life.
There's no blame, I might be doing the same,
It's a state of mind.

So buck the conditioning
Resist genderization.
Question conformity
And never give in.

Returning From the Sea

Hear waves crash or trickle,
On the sand. Warm or cold,
Always new but old, old.
Big and blue, small and white.
Smell the salt, taste the spray
Feel motion forever.

Summer, it's ideal, cool
Winter, unpredictable
Rough, swirly, freezing,
Overflowing, ceaseless,
Unfriendly, grey and big.
Stay away, stay away.

Visit on away days,
Difference from the norm,
Freedom and space beckon,
Sand manipulative,
Water unstoppable,
Home tired and satisfied.

Leave the unknowable.
Home equals solidness
Friendly, familiar,
Dependable and there.
Not unknowable or
Different every time
You open the curtains.

Guitar

The long smooth, dark, silky neck
Leading to a golden, flat, shiny body.
The fine grain of the wood in line
With the brass wound strings.
The curvaceous sides offering a roundness
Which echoes, resonating and emanating
From the sound hole at waist level
Like a chord from an open umbilicus.

Above

You were above me when I was small
And you were tall

Above in stature
Above in knowledge.

You knew wrong from right
And taught me left from it.

You were below me in height
To my sight;

Below me in learning
Below me in dexterity

But you knew things that were above you
And perhaps still do.

He should have been beside me
An equal partner

To take his share
To make it fair.

But he was unable
He wasn't stable.

Techno Canticle

Birds and butterflies, blooms in blue,
The warm summer sun shining through.
Leaves in tall trees
Playing to the breeze
And a dog barks an octave higher.
Engineered combustion underpins
The natural symphony, fleeting
And speeds past, ignoring the rhythm
Presented by the world modulation
With nature.

The Mystical Road Home

The road home, very long
Driving on and on.
Along the road are monsters,
One friendly and green,
There are others, unseen.

My friendly monster, green
In summer with it's coat on,
Brown and veiny in winter
Still swinging it's trunk
Swaying, drunk?

And further down the road, a cloud
Also green,
Tethered to the ground by a stalk,
It can't walk.
Along and along, where is this home I'm heading for,
And when I find it, will there be a door?
And what about the monsters, will they let me past?

There's a monster called poverty, invisible,
But strong enough to chain me down.
And another called boredom, like a leach
Sucking out the sparks of enthusiasm.

Journey on and slay the monsters,
What will my excalibur be?
Keep on searching, never resting
Until at last I'm home and free.

Solitude While Travelling

Encased in my car
I can go far.
The pull of the road
Draws me from my abode.
But segregated in my metallic bubble,
Unable to share happiness or trouble.

Communication with other beings
Is lost in speed and rules of travel,
The only people that I see
Travel south if I head north.

No wonder the conversations of travel
Consist of repetitive questions
How far, how fast, was it busy,
Was it quiet, nice run? etc etc.

The questions are made on arrival,
And referred to again on leaving,
A pragmatic conversation repeated
Hence knowledge of travel is shared.

But it would take a monumental shift
To change in habit and drift
To commute people together
To experience the weather
To experience the same
To know another's name.

But perhaps it's just too much to ask
To veer from the present task,
Of going from A to B in time
Not connecting with another mind.

Do we continue as we are?
Individuals in a car,
Or can we stop and change direction
Allow ourselves the benefit of flexion.

Rural night

Staccato sounds
Short and sharp
But wooden, hollow
In the dark.

Where is it from?
Outside, disembodied
I think, disturbing
Unsettling.

Premiered to me
The night symphony,
Stilted yet wrap around
These strange to me sounds.

Penetrating and awesome,
I hear an echo
But it's coming from elsewhere
This answering call.

Their cries through night sky
Connecting the two.
How wondrous these sounds.
And I – close the window.

The Rites of Passage Trilogy

Discovering her body

Her promiscuity excites her,
Her breath and pulse quicken.
The freshness and novelty make her attentive,
Her eyes darken, she feels earthy,
There's harmony and beauty in the act she once feared.

Daddy dear

She sees him quite clearly now the mist has lifted
He's not next to God – he's just a man,
Using mens' ways to appear knowledgeable and superior,
His fragility, his ego nurtured by her
Yes he's kind and obliging and knows well some things,
But the font of all knowledge isn't him,
He's human and fallible and more approachable now.

Arriving

She's o.k. she has decided
With her achievements so far.
There's no way she could ever
Be what they wanted.
Of their expectations she fails time after time.
But she's o.k. as she is.
There's no need to continue
The uphill struggle for their approval,
She can live as she likes,
It really won't matter
She can set her own standards,
Live by her rules.

Mindscape

Mindscape, how does it look?
Now it's flat and calm,
Earlier it was rocky, dark and dangerous.

Mindscape, escape
Into or out of it.
Easy to escape into
But out of – is it possible?

Escape into daydreams, trances and meditation,
Escape should be inscape from
Drudgery and boredom.

But how is it possible to escape from the mind?
From the worries and stresses
The nightmares.

Exploring a mindscape, scary,
Not like reading a picture.
It isn't framed, it doesn't end.

Ideas thief

This daemon steals ideas,
Hides them in a black hole,
Mischievous fellow.
Makes good inventive ideas invisible
And forces a reliance on habit:
He promotes uncreativity
In his brown/grey drab world.

Ideas should bubble up,
Be lively, with energy.
But he kidnaps them –
Before they have chance
To come alive.

There are an army of daemons,
Which should be obliterated.
They stop human advancement.

Having identified him,
He must be destroyed.
How? He is illusive.
By head clearing, get rid of the block.
Make new space to explore,
Banish negativity.

Then, no longer can he sap your creativity,
Let those ideas root and flower.
Give them a chance, enhance your life.
Make space for you,
To yourself be true,
Get the bugger and press delete.

Beautiful bed

To be,
In bed.
Thoughts roam.
Wonder where I'll go,
Give my thoughts free flight,
But take me along tonight.

Beautiful bed,
Safe bed.
My boat in a sea of thoughts.
Absolutely unsinkable.
Voyage of discovery,
Find me a lovery.

Beautiful bed.
I can think the most daring thoughts,
And no one even knows.
It's my true escape.
It's where I plant my thought seeds,
Where I plan spiritual deeds.

Beautiful bed,
Disappear beneath the covers.
The place of passion,
And inspiration.
It's the place to be,
When there's just me.

Vivaldi's 4 Seasons

Vivaldi's four seasons describe
Vividly, and let you hide inside
The senses and feelings that it invokes,
You fly and glide and hover and smoke.

Spring shoots triumphant.
Treble sounds, jubilant.
Colours, bold and basic,
Mood, mad and manic.

Summer, full grown and confident,
Colours subtle, sounds content,
Scents balmy and heavy,
Base notes chase high sounds in harmony.

Autumn, job done and leaving,
Flying away, knowing and prancing,
Colours definite and flamey,
Sounds smooth and arty.

Winter, piercing, probing and precise,
Coping with hardships – on ice,
Sounds high, brittle and thin,
Let a new life cycle begin.

Daemon of Doubt

Daemon of Doubt lurks,
Waiting, ready...
In the nondescript byways of your mind,
She will do her worst.

She gracefully lets Doubt seep into your thoughts,
Unnoticed, just waiting,
At the edge of your consciousness.
Distrust being born.

She dislikes activity,
Positiveness is her enemy,
Indecision she likes,
Waiting is her game.

But we can eliminate her,
Be positive, have confidence,
Self belief will defy her,
Enthusiasm and goodwill defeat her.

For the lack of a quack

A small brush on high hat
Is the sound of ice breaking
As ducks swim through
In the extrovert morning sun.

A respite from social manipulation,
They need no assessment
No questioning or judgement
Just pragmatic arrangements.

A simple society is that of the duck
With which our complex language
Lacks a suitable rhyme –
But a fuck is probably what I need
And a ruck has similar connotations
And I'm pissed off with my job.

A duck can take flight.

Desirability

Desirability
It's good to know
That I am still
Fancyable.

Someone to talk with, and
Understand, and
Enjoy a laugh, when all
Else is grumpy.

You're not turned off by me.
I lust your attention
Kiss me, kiss me
You're touch is awesome.

My confidence is high.
And thanks to you
I now know that
I can still pull
Even from a wheelchair.

Coffee broken

The other day I felt fed up
And so I made myself a cup
Of coffee, and ate a chocky bicky.

Now I'm fed up, stressed out
And attending Weight Watchers.

Inebriate Observations

Like a bubble in a glass of beer
I'd like to rise to the top.
I've always had this urge in me,
But to the top of what?

Head way

Now I'm making head way,
There's room for me to be,
Dispel the over casting cloud
And let the force flow free.

Zinning and unfogged
My mind alive and alert,
Open to new ideas
Able to deal with fears.

Thought processes freed,
It's up to me to guide my life,
I have many choices now,
There's no shackles and no strife.

My plans are valid,
They are my plans for me,
They are fluid and moveable,
Exciting and doable.

Rainbow

A message from the universe,
Communicates through sun and rain.
Growing now, broadening,
Adding colour to our lives.

Light passing through rain drops,
Colours separated as wavelengths bend them differently,
Making our world bright.

Colour emanates from clouded skies,
Another mystery of our world.
Nature makes magic happen,
What right do we have to change it?

Slugduggery

Invaders of my garden,
Cradle snatchers of the earth,
Snatching baby plants,
At their time of birth.

They invade by night,
Leaving their tell tale trail,
Shoots that had just emerged,
Food for slugs and snails.

There must be an army of them,
Watching for seeds to pop up,
Waiting for new leaves to sprout
And disappearing before sun up.

They cause endless worry,
Perhaps I should sit up all night,
To catch them devouring seedlings,
And cause them a bit of a fright.

But how to out wit them,
The struggle goes on and on.
There seems to be no solution,
I just want a kind conclusion.

Rhythms of the World

Rhythms of the world,
Rhythms of the night,
Listen, listen
To the rhythm of life.

Let the rhythm rock you,
Let the rhythm sway you,
Reverberating, thrumming, let it move your soul.

The beat can stir you,
Tempo fast or slow,
Listen, hear it
Silently move you.

Let the rhythm rock you,
Let the rhythm sway you
Jangling, echoing, let it move your soul.

Some rhythms last, the rumba
Some more personal, in speech,
Listen, hear it –
The rhythm in the air.

Let the rhythm rock you,
Let the rhythm sway you,
Undulating, swinging, let it move your soul.

Printed in the United Kingdom by
Lightning Source UK Ltd., Milton Keynes
139427UK00002B/19/P